Contents

Introduction 2

Chapter 1 Creating a Culture of Privacy...3

Chapter 2 Understanding and Prioritizing Data Privacy 8

Chapter 3 Implementing a Privacy, Risk, and Assurance Program 16

Chapter 4 Data Classification and Inventory 32

Chapter 5 Data Sharing...46

Introduction

Is your company handling personal data? Safeguarding privacy is crucial in the digital age. To effectively address this, establish a "culture of privacy" within your organization. We will guide you on why privacy matters, creating a program aligned with corporate values, fostering privacy advocates, integrating privacy into the product life cycle, and measuring a lasting culture of privacy. Ready to shape your organization's response to this critical issue?

Data and the information are vital for individuals, organizations, and governments. It plays a critical role in delivering services, products, and experiences to individuals, fostering positive and forward-looking interactions between citizens and the government. The key questions include: How do we utilize, explore, extract value from, and safeguard data? The challenge is to innovate within a data-centric future while preserving our cultural values.

Facing fines of up to 4% of revenue, negative headlines, and loss of customer trust due to privacy breaches can be a PR disaster and lead to legal troubles. We'll design a comprehensive privacy program, covering historical context, the evolving data landscape, big data's impact, legal changes, and customer expectations. We'll craft a unique, modern privacy strategy, including executive sponsorship, team structure, data governance, privacy tools, and metrics. This book is for everyone—engineers, product managers, attorneys, security/compliance specialists, executives—to equip you for a role in your company's privacy program.

Companies and governments amass vast amounts of sensitive data, analyzed by numerous engineers to create products and generate revenue. This data is often shared across systems and teams. To ensure responsible handling and prevent harm to customers, companies must establish a robust data governance strategy. Privacy, rooted in transparency and trust, is crucial. I'll guide you in initiating your governance program through data classification and inventory.

Industry professionals often view data from the perspective of enhancing features, increasing engagement, and driving profits. Many online activities, including personalization, ads, and payments, heavily rely on data sharing. However, legitimate concerns and malicious actors pose risks, especially considering the vast amount of data collected and the nuanced nature of privacy risk. This book aims to guide you in sharing data while prioritizing both trust and compliance. I will assist you in integrating privacy measures into your data sharing practices, allowing you to leverage the advantages of data while minimizing risks.

Chapter 1 Creating a Culture of Privacy

Building a culture of privacy

Privacy is a frequently discussed topic, with concerns ranging from companies to the government knowing personal details. The meaning of privacy varies based on factors like ethnicity, gender, and nationality. In Europe, it's considered a fundamental human right, protecting personal data through legal justification. In the US, it's often defined as the right to be left alone, choosing not to share personal information. In Asia, privacy involves hiding one's identity. Technological advancements constantly shape our privacy expectations, and the culture of privacy within organizations should adapt to changing norms. We'll focus on safeguarding personal data, including information that can identify individuals, and creating a privacy-centric organizational culture.

Why organizations need to think about building a culture of privacy

Every action in our digital lives generates a data trail accessible to companies, creating both opportunities and responsibilities. Initially, privacy was often overlooked during the internet's early days. Today, the proliferation of data-collecting technologies demands that every company prioritizes privacy. Three key reasons include: 1) Building and maintaining customer trust, which requires transparent communication about data handling; 2) Impact on the bottom line, as a failure to collect data properly may limit future use and affect company valuation; 3) Employees pose a significant privacy risk if unaware or indifferent to the company's privacy stance. Establishing a culture where privacy is integral to every employee's role is crucial for long-term success in the digital age.

New privacy regulations on the horizon

Privacy has deep historical roots, emerging as a legal right in the US Constitution's Fourth Amendment. Early US legal thinkers, like Louis Brandeis and Samuel Warren, defined privacy as "the right to be let alone." In the US, diverse laws protect privacy in various domains, such as health, education, children's, video viewing, and financial data. European privacy laws, spurred by post-World War II concerns, culminated in the Data Protection Directive in 1995 and the General Data Protection Regulation (GDPR) in 2016, extending rights globally. The GDPR applies not only to EU-based companies but also to any entity processing EU residents' data, with potential fines reaching 4% of global annual turnover. Asia, Latin America, and other regions are increasingly enacting and enforcing privacy regulations. Understanding and complying with these laws is crucial for companies operating globally.

Consumers are taking notice of privacy

Privacy was traditionally seen as a risk mitigation issue, focused on avoiding breaches and regulatory scrutiny. Consumers were generally indifferent, willingly exchanging data for free services. Executives urged people to share more, dismissing privacy concerns. Despite privacy scandals, online platforms like Facebook and Google thrived. However, shifts occurred as people became more aware of the data, they generate daily. Technological advancements, such as the iPhone, Facebook, AI, cloud computing, and IoT, contributed to this data explosion. Snowden's revelations in 2013 exposed global surveillance programs, prompting individuals to question data collection, privacy control, and demand transparency. Companies embracing transparency in data practices gain a competitive edge by building trust and loyalty in the era of big data.

Assessing your current privacy program

To establish a culture of privacy, start by designating a privacy champion within your organization, preferably a Chief Privacy Officer. Ensure they have the authority, resources, and visibility to lead privacy efforts. Develop essential documentation, including a privacy policy and a data breach plan. Implement a privacy notice for employees, clarifying data handling and their rights. Conduct a comprehensive gap assessment to identify personal information, assess controls, and gauge compliance. Establish a process for reviewing and documenting privacy risks in product development. Appoint a privacy leader, create documentation, inform employees, conduct a gap assessment, and integrate privacy into product reviews.

Why a privacy policy is not enough

In the digital age, nearly every company gathers personal data from customers, necessitating a strategic approach to privacy. Merely relying on legal and IT departments is insufficient as privacy is a company-wide strategic issue. Establishing a culture of privacy ensures that every employee comprehends their role in upholding privacy commitments and overall data strategy. Failure in privacy considerations can lead to customer loss, profit reduction, negative press, and missed business opportunities. Developing a sustainable culture of privacy involves addressing trade-offs, determining data collection limits, improving communication with customers, and navigating ethical challenges to create innovative products while respecting privacy. Companies grappling with these complexities are on the path to long-term success.

Making privacy a brand differentiator

Cloud computing, artificial intelligence, and the Internet of Things, constant data generation prompts individuals and businesses to make trust decisions when engaging online. Building a culture of privacy becomes a unique opportunity for organizations, serving as a brand differentiator that communicates trustworthiness to customers. As the interconnected world intensifies privacy concerns, companies should invest in transparency, going beyond mere reliance on privacy policies. It's essential to engage with customers creatively, communicate clearly about data practices, and establish robust measures for handling breaches. Companies that prioritize privacy not only gain customer loyalty but also unlock opportunities for innovative solutions and business models by fostering trust and obtaining valuable insights from customer data. Privacy should be ingrained as a fundamental business practice, equivalent to customer service, across all industries in the digital economy.

Tying privacy to your corporate mission

Many employees in companies are unfamiliar with or feel disconnected from the concept of privacy, as it is often briefly mentioned in annual business conduct training. To thrive in the digital era, companies must reshape their approach to privacy by fostering an organizational environment where every employee prioritizes customer privacy. This involves aligning the importance of privacy with corporate values. Even if a company seemingly has no direct connection to privacy, such as a manufacturer of athletic wear, it can establish a link by considering its mission. For example, if the company's goal is to help people get fit and lead better lives, ensuring customer trust in data protection becomes crucial. By incorporating these values into privacy policies and decision-making frameworks, companies can demonstrate that safeguarding customer data is integral to achieving their core mission, going beyond legal obligations. This approach encourages employees to view privacy as an essential element of the company's identity and purpose.

Selling privacy to the executive team

After aligning your company's mission and values with privacy, the next challenging step is gaining executive buy-in and disseminating the message throughout the organization. Executive teams often perceive privacy as a defensive task rather than an opportunity. To shift this mindset, it's essential to demonstrate how privacy adds value to the company. Highlighting market differentiation, customer loyalty, and talent attraction can illustrate the strategic importance of privacy. Several tech companies, such as Apple and Microsoft, have successfully differentiated their brands by emphasizing privacy. Customer loyalty is fostered by maintaining privacy promises, and a strong approach to privacy can attract top talent, as people prefer working for and with companies that prioritize privacy. Once you've established the link between privacy, corporate values, and the company's success, seek executive support to evangelize this message throughout the organization.

Making privacy relevant to every employee

Building a culture of privacy takes time and requires everyone in the organization to work toward a common goal with a shared framework. To transition from a concept to a pervasive culture, actions speak louder than words. Making privacy relatable is crucial, as employees often struggle to understand complex policies. Creating awareness through events, such as movie screenings, inviting speakers, or hosting educational activities like lock picking, can simplify the topic. Make the company's approach to data privacy easy to understand by distilling it into key concepts or phrases, like LinkedIn's three C's: Clarity, Consistency, and Control. Connect privacy to the overall mission and values of the company, with executives directly communicating this to employees. Provide clear guidance on data collection, use, and storage boundaries, offering training to different teams and encouraging questions. Making privacy relatable and providing a simple mandate helps instill privacy awareness throughout the organization.

Building a team of privacy champions

Once you've established the fundamentals of a privacy program, the next step is building a culture with advocates who understand and promote it. Identify teams with shared interests, such as security, compliance, internal audit, and legal. Create a privacy champion program involving employees from various departments. To incentivize participation, tie completion to career advancement, bonuses, or recognition programs. Develop a comprehensive course covering privacy basics, company policies, and procedures over three to six months. Encourage participants to discuss real privacy issues and propose solutions. Treat course alumni as valued members, recognizing them at events and providing ongoing updates through newsletters. Cultivate relationships with other teams and nurture your community of champions, building a network to identify and address privacy issues throughout the organization.

Making privacy everyone's job

Privacy is often seen as a concern for legal or compliance teams, resulting in companies with excellent policies but lacking a true privacy culture. To engage employees across various departments, encourage them to empathize with customers and recognize their responsibility as guardians of customer data. Emphasize that they should treat this data with the same care they expect for their own. The benefits include employees becoming ambassadors for the company's commitment to privacy, reducing the risk of privacy violations, and enhancing the company's appeal to talent in security and engineering. Building a robust privacy program requires every employee to view and integrate privacy as a fundamental aspect of their job.

Creating a set of privacy guidelines for the business

To truly establish a culture of privacy, operationalizing it is crucial. This involves creating documentation that outlines principles for making tough decisions and enlisting leaders across the organization to support and enforce these principles. Address nuanced questions that arise from pushing boundaries, such as using data for certain purposes or responding to government requests. Establish internal principles, document them with executive support, and distribute them to senior leadership. Conduct workshops to internalize these guidelines. Additionally, form an internal privacy council comprising executives from core teams, including a C-Suite member, to meet quarterly, address privacy issues, and provide perspectives. This council helps align business goals with privacy principles and avoids inconsistent approaches, ensuring a unified and compliant privacy stance.

Building privacy into your products

Operationalizing a culture of privacy involves integrating privacy into the product development cycle, a concept known as privacy by design. This entails asking fundamental privacy questions during project initiation, such as the data collected, its use, and access. To ensure ongoing privacy consideration, embed a privacy expert, ideally a lawyer or engineer, in projects with privacy impact. Alternatively, implement a privacy champion program to train individuals throughout the organization. Establish guiding rules for common privacy issues and encourage teams to think about user experience, including opt-in and opt-out choices. Before product launch, implement a gating process where security and privacy teams sign off to ensure regulatory compliance and alignment with privacy values. The key takeaway is to prioritize privacy from the outset, avoiding it as an afterthought in product development.

Sustaining a culture of privacy

To ensure a lasting culture of privacy, implement regular measurements and metrics for your privacy program. Track customer inquiries, privacy policy engagement, regulator inquiries, and data incidents. Conduct annual audits, including random employee interviews, to assess program effectiveness. Establish an engaging and mandatory training program for all employees, with consequences for non-compliance. Stay attuned to customer sentiments by monitoring inquiries and complaints, and consider focus groups for deeper insights. Recognize and reward employees for outstanding privacy efforts, integrating privacy into the annual review process. Keep employees informed with a monthly newsletter on privacy topics. Finally, celebrate achievements with events, reports to executives and the board, and internal promotions, appreciating the ethical work of preserving customer data access.

Chapter 2 Understanding and Prioritizing Data Privacy

Privacy overview

Data privacy and security are universal concerns that impact every industry and individual. Personal data, such as healthcare information, family details, and location, significantly influence individuals. Beyond personal considerations, questions arise about how people connect in space and time, control who has access to their whereabouts, and create spaces for privacy and creativity. The concept of authorized information sharing extends from individual decisions to larger groups, encompassing classrooms, students evaluating information quality, and citizens grappling with complex issues like immigration and national security. Decisions at every level are shaped by data stories and individual narratives, forming the foundation of human experiences. Understanding and innovating in the realm of data is thus a shared interest that transcends various aspects of society.

Data tells a story

Data serves as a narrative, with our daily activities contributing to this story. Whether it's requesting a playlist, rerouting using GPS, or sharing photos online, every interaction with devices and sensors adds to the collective narrative. The multitude of devices, from traffic lights to cameras, captures various aspects of our lives. The impact of these data stories ranges from ephemeral observations to more permanent records, influencing our experiences in both personal and professional spheres. In essence, data consistently tells the story of each individual.

Data as intellectual property

Data can be likened to other forms of intellectual property, such as trademarks, copyrights, and patents, as it represents the fruits of creative and inventive processes. While data may not be owned in the same way as physical property, it possesses aspects of ownership. The way data flows, is shared, processed, and handled involves considerations of ownership. Viewing data in the context of intellectual property means recognizing its potential to be leveraged, to cause harm, to build value, and to have ethical implications. Unlike a neutral zone, where data has no impact, data is inherently linked to intellectual property, and its collection and handling present opportunities for protection, ethical treatment, or misuse. Data is not a zero-sum game; it always carries the potential for positive or negative consequences based on how it is managed.

Personally identifiable information

Privacy and data protection, as per my definition, involve the authorized processing of personally identifiable data based on fair principles. Personally identifiable information (PII) refers to data that, either alone or in combination with other elements, can uniquely describe an individual. An analogy to clarify is the use of a common name like "Michael," which, when linked to a specific person, becomes private and personally identifiable. Notably, the concept of secrecy is not integral to PII; it's more about the processing of the information. The challenge in defining PII lies in its expanding scope as our data capabilities grow. Information that was once purely observational can now, when combined with other data elements, identify an individual.

Privacy vs. secrecy

Privacy differs from secrecy, a distinction that is often overlooked. Cultural backgrounds also influence how individuals perceive privacy. Privacy involves the authorized processing of personally identifiable information, which may or may not be kept secret. Secrecy and confidentiality are not synonymous with privacy. For instance, sharing credit card information for a purchase is a privacy issue, and violating it involves using the information for purposes other than payment. Conversely, publicly sharing non-secret information, such as being a keynote speaker at a conference, still falls under privacy regulations even though it's not confidential. Understanding this distinction is crucial for effective data governance.

Moral, legal, and ethical systems

A well-governed data system is based on four key elements. Firstly, the processing must be moral, avoiding actions that may be ethically questionable, such as extreme measures like chipping prisoners. Secondly, the processing must be ethical, aligning with the brand and consistent treatment that is deemed appropriate. Thirdly, it must be legal, adhering to rules, regulations, and local requirements applicable to the data. Finally, the processing must be fair, considering principles like the Fair Information Protection Principles (FIPPs), which assess the proportionality of information collection and its lifecycle. Going through this framework ensures a comprehensive evaluation of the data system's morality, ethics, legality, and fairness.

The individual's perspective

Aggregate data tells stories about communities and cultures, revealing both value and potential disruptions. Understanding and protecting data are crucial aspects of navigating its dynamic movement. Data serves as a mirror reflecting humanity, capturing the history of daily lives, and contributing to the betterment of societies for future generations. Whether it's planning daily activities or attending significant events like a child's school play, data plays a vital role in facilitating and enhancing various aspects of individual lives.

The organization's perspective

Organizations value data privacy and data because it brings significant value to their operations. Despite some organizations thinking they don't care about it yet; the importance of data has been downplayed due to the perception that it is a cheap and easily accessible commodity. However, data is a fundamental asset that aids in hiring, customer relations, product development, business growth, communication with investors, and maintaining data security. Forward-thinking organizations recognize the crucial role of data, treating it as a valuable asset, much like currency, with careful consideration for its protection and utilization.

Privacy is contextual

Privacy and private information can be perceived differently by individuals depending on the situation. For instance, when planning a surprise party, contextual cues, such as the location and time, are selectively shared. This small example illustrates how contextualization varies across different use cases, emphasizing the importance of understanding the context in which personally identifiable information is shared, such as with a doctor versus coworkers, as data naturally flows through various aspects of one's life.

Trust and integrity

Building trust in systems and organizations is crucial, achieved by ensuring that systems are designed and operated with the best interests in mind. This involves owning, operating, and governing systems in a trustworthy manner, with accountability for information throughout its lifecycle. Organizations can establish trust by conducting audits to identify weaknesses and strengths, ensuring systems process information ethically, morally, and legally. Trust is earned over time through understanding data, its intended purpose, and consistently supporting it with people, process, and technology. Regular testing and quality assurance are essential in generating and maintaining trust, extending beyond the brand name to the individual's data transactions over time. This forms the essence of trust in data protection systems.

Consumer trust cliff

The "data trust cliff" is a real phenomenon marked by a sudden loss of trust after a breach or violation in a data relationship. This decline occurs when individuals feel their information has been over-shared, not used as agreed, or subjected to excessive collection and observation. Trust cliffs can result from security breaches or unexpected sharing, creating a challenging situation for organizations as they must rebuild trust after a significant loss.

Consumers want transparency

Consumers seek transparency regarding the collection, processing, and use of their information. They prefer straightforward communication over lengthy, complex legal policies. Transparency, for them, extends beyond knowing what is done; they want to understand the actions taken in response to their data concerns. Providing accessible channels for questions and corrections is crucial for complete transparency. Transparency is context-specific; for instance, when downloading a photo-editing app, users want to know where their photos are stored, whether the app accesses other images, and if information will be shared after the transaction. Offering clear, consistent, and honest communication is essential for establishing trust with consumers.

Protecting the story

When a data-built story is lost or altered, several consequences may occur. Goods and services may not meet expectations, leading to a loss of integrity in systems and potential damage to both organizations and individuals. The damage can result in monetary penalties, but more significantly, it can impact integrity and trust, making it challenging for consumers to trust that a system tells accurate and fair stories over time. Inaccurate data stories can hinder third parties, legal advisors, and financial advisors in their roles, affecting an organization's growth and decision-making. The multiplier effect of data loss extends beyond individual repercussions, affecting organizations' abilities to thrive and grow based on datasets and insights. The economic impact on employees, especially in highly competitive fields like Silicon Valley, emphasizes the importance of protecting datasets and information for the benefit of individuals, organizations, and society as a whole.

Vulnerability to a system

In the privacy context, vulnerability differs from the security world's understanding. It's not just the surface of attack; instead, it's a shared vulnerability between the individual providing information and the organization processing it. This vulnerability involves concerns about correct sharing, processing, and ensuring the narrative aligns with the intended story. Despite this vulnerability, there's an opportunity to build trust and a data asset over time, expanding the narrative across various product sets and new markets. However, the constant balance exists in collecting enough information for safety, law enforcement, and civic good without overly invasive practices, such as unwanted advertisements or manipulative actions based on gathered data.

Data in the wrong hands

Every day, news headlines report data breaches, losses, and vulnerabilities. When an attack occurs, poorly governed and curated data becomes its own vulnerability. The major concerns in data breaches involve knowing, willful, and criminal activities, particularly hackers aiming for financial gain or power. These digital criminals' traffic stolen information on the black market, assuming false identities, and exploiting the integrity of innocent individuals' data stories. Motivations often revolve around greed and power, with nation-states seeking advantages and individuals profiting from citizens' valuable and intact data stories. It's not just a technological glitch; it's a crime.

React to privacy issues

In the event of a breach or data theft, proactive measures are crucial. Conduct tabletop exercises, envision various scenarios of data misuse, and prepare your team for efficient responses. Run through different possibilities, such as vendor mishaps or attacks through third parties. Rehearse these scenarios before an actual incident occurs, ensuring that your team is well-prepared. Discovering a breach requires facing it like any systemic risk to your business. Consider the context, assessing the impact on individuals and the organization. Think about data in a contextual and meaningful way, focusing on people, processes, and technology simultaneously. Coordinate with technical teams to halt the breach, protect vulnerable areas, and understand potential product vulnerabilities. Legal obligations may require notifying authorities based on the incident's impact and location. The complexities of responding to an incident make prevention, governance, and robust architecture critical, helping save time, resources, and intellectual capital when the inevitable occurs.

Information economy

The information economy is thriving and becoming more accessible to numerous organizations. It enables individuals to establish and benefit from their information economies. To minimize risks in this economy, focus on addressing liabilities like vulnerabilities, patching holes, and preventing data loss. The information economy functions similarly to any other economy, maintaining a balance between assets (data, stories, communication) and fostering enriched relationships, whether with employees or customers. Despite risks, investing wisely in data, educating governance teams, promoting transparency, and creating a consumer-friendly environment contribute to a data economy that yields unimaginable dividends over time. Treat data as a form of currency, understanding its power lies in what it can enable – insights, business direction, stakeholder satisfaction, and overall organizational success. The goal of the data economy is to transform information into wisdom, utilizing gathered, processed, and shared data transactions for a clear understanding of the present, importance, and insights derived from daily interactions.

Trust, transparency, and accountability

Organizations dealing with data, privacy, security, and data assets should follow a strategic, phased approach akin to setting up a business or implementing new features. Initiating with a scoping workshop is crucial to identify the business problem, human factors, and desired outcomes driven by data assets. Understanding the data assets needed, their combinations, and the system's impact is essential. Moving on to the "who" involves identifying all players, including users, decision-makers, and groups interacting with the information-based system. Evaluating existing tools, technologies, infrastructure, and legal aspects provides a foundation. Creating a process diagram details how individuals interact with data over time. This planning process, although thorough, doesn't need to be lengthy and can significantly enhance the long-term value and efficiency of the system, ensuring it aligns with business requirements.

Planning for data

When preparing for data activities, whether as an organization or an individual, it's essential to approach it like planning a trip. Just as you plan for a journey by selecting a vehicle, cleaning it, filling it with gas, securing it, and setting a destination, organizations must similarly plan for collecting valuable data about individuals. Many organizations amass large volumes of data without a clear destination, which lacks business sense, violates human rights, is legally questionable, and poses risks. Planning, understanding technology capabilities, and assessing the need for new technology are crucial steps in managing data as a critical asset in the digital age.

Privacy engineering

Privacy engineering, grounded in the broad concept of engineering, extends beyond computer science or hardware and involves using available tools, resources, and math to systematically solve problems. In the context of privacy engineering, the focus is on designing and creating privacy from the outset, aligning with the concept of privacy by design. This approach emphasizes authorized processing of personally identifiable information in accordance with moral, legal, ethical, and fair principles. Organizations committed to information-centric, data-centric, and privacy-centric systems often adopt a privacy-by-design policy. Privacy engineering encompasses problem-solving, tool utilization, planning, architecture, testing, transparency, and accountability structures to support the implementation of privacy by design.

Moral crumple zones

"Moral crumple zones" is a concept developed by Dr. Madeleine Elish. Similar to the safety approach in vehicle design, where crumple zones absorb impact energy, a moral and ethical crumple zone in data collection considers the known unknowns in information usage. It involves categorizing potential ethical challenges, such as over-collection, over-sharing, lack of accountability, and transparency loss. The goal is to design flexible systems that enable authorized sharing of personally identifiable information in a fair, moral, legal, and ethical manner.

Culture of privacy

Creating a privacy culture involves building the habit and muscle of privacy within an organization. It's not solely the responsibility of the Chief Privacy Officer; rather, it involves all individuals—employees, customers, and third parties. Each person should understand the importance of data privacy, what it means for them and the business, and how they contribute to it in their role. To begin building a privacy culture, individuals can create a top 10 list of important information, identify actions to enhance data protection, and share responsibilities. Regardless of job title or authority, everyone can make a meaningful impact on privacy within the organization.

Innovation

Innovation is pervasive in today's data landscape, and the phrase "how we've always done it" represents an impediment to progress in the information economy. In the context of privacy engineering, innovation involves scrutinizing each level of the process, solutioning, and accountability to achieve transparency and profitability. Whether it's redefining identity management, fractalizing data for contextual use, exploring quantum encryption beyond current paradigms, or creating new roles like privacy officers, there are numerous opportunities for innovation. Collaborative efforts from diverse fields, including engineering, mathematics, law, psychology, and the arts, are essential to shaping a sustainable and person-centric data economy. Innovation beckons for those interested in profiting from and enhancing the data economy, fostering a space where everyone's unique skills contribute to envisioning the next steps for our economy and culture.

Emerging technologies

The initial 30 years of innovation were about making things work as instructed by pioneers. In the next 30 years, we have the autonomy to shape how machines interact with us. Current innovations like blockchain, the Internet of Things, ubiquitous surveillance, and data-centric changes in work, education, and play offer a glimpse into the future. Instead of passively accepting an impending data deluge, we can proactively innovate using privacy engineering to focus on the purpose behind data collection. By contemplating business outcomes, cultural growth, societal relationships, and understanding differences, we can steer the direction of data and innovation. Recognizing that data artifacts will transform over time, akin to personal perspectives evolving, privacy engineering allows us to manage and comprehend the evolving nature of data trails, ensuring alignment with desired futures.

Chapter 3 Implementing a Privacy, Risk, and Assurance Program

Why you need a cross-functional privacy program

People typically don't read online privacy policies and terms of use. In their high-growth phase, the company faced challenges managing privacy policies for multiple apps and acquisitions globally. Insufficient legal resources and engineers hard-coding policies led to a critical incident where users received the wrong policies. This incident, though pre-dating today's strict privacy laws, taught us the importance of cross-functional privacy approaches, emphasizing collaboration and organization across teams and markets. The lesson is that even well-intentioned engineers can make costly privacy mistakes, highlighting the need for a more structured, cross-disciplinary privacy strategy. Note: I am not an attorney, and none of this should be considered legal advice.

What does privacy mean and how does it relate to security?

Defining privacy can be challenging, but in a business context, it focuses on authorized, fair, and legitimate processing of personal information, prioritizing the end user's perspective. The International Association of Privacy Professionals emphasizes user control over personal information. Security, on the other hand, involves cybersecurity strategies preventing unauthorized access to organizational assets like computers, networks, and data, ensuring integrity and confidentiality. While good security is crucial for privacy, privacy involves deeper considerations between different data relationships. Tensions can arise between security and privacy, highlighting the nuanced challenges in real-world operations.

A history of privacy

Greg Ferenstein provides a detailed history of privacy, spanning from ancient Greece to the present day. Privacy, as we understand it now, emerged around 150 years ago, evolving from an elite concept to a mainstream expectation. During the Gilded Age, homes became symbols of privacy, but access was largely dependent on wealth. Legislative measures, such as the 1710 Post Office Act and the 1903 penalty for unauthorized likeness use, reflected evolving privacy concerns. The post-1950s era saw a growing fear of a world without privacy, with the 1960s marking the norm of individualized phones and private spaces. In the 2000s, privacy became a competition between the desire for identity and anonymity. In 2019, a meeting in Israel highlighted privacy as a balance between these human impulses. Recent studies suggest that customers care about privacy but may lack context or time for informed decisions, leading to information avoidance. Understanding this history is crucial for developing a comprehensive privacy strategy in today's context.

How we got to this moment

Many individuals distrust large institutions and question their operational models. Addressing concerns raised by skeptics involves explaining how companies make money, especially those offering free services, and understanding the paradox of leading tech companies with smart engineers facing significant privacy issues. Reflecting on my experience over a decade ago as a hands-on engineer, the traditional top-down, centralized working model prioritized control and minimized privacy or security issues but hindered innovation. A shift occurred towards a bottom-up, decentralized model, empowering engineers, allowing rapid prototyping, and rewarding individual product development. Cloud providers facilitated data storage but complicated centralized endeavors like privacy and security. Simultaneously, changes on the demand side, driven by widespread internet use and connected devices, led to high expectations for personalized, fast-working products, resulting in extensive data collection. This seemed effective until the surge in data volume led to privacy harms. The relationship between a company's business success and its privacy obligations becomes apparent, creating tension between customer engagement, innovation, and privacy and security concerns. The convergence of smaller changes has contributed to the current landscape.

Data: Risks and rewards

Privacy is crucial due to our heavy reliance on data collected by companies from users. The tech boom and bust and the great recession underscore the importance of understanding trends and market needs. Big data, a product and output of technology innovation, presents a significant privacy challenge. While it empowers businesses with valuable insights, it also poses risks, notably data breaches and the potential weaponization of sensitive personal data. The Equifax breach, exposing vast amounts of personal information, resulted in substantial financial losses and a downgrade by Moody's, citing cybersecurity and privacy concerns. The OPM breach, involving sensitive government personnel files, demonstrated how combining datasets could lead to national security risks. Investing in privacy is essential to mitigate these risks and protect against severe consequences, as seen in these real-life cases.

Privacy: Trust and safety

Corporate leaders often view privacy as a compliance task tied to laws, which poses challenges due to the extensive reach of privacy regulations. Beyond potential fines, the bureaucratic processes imposed by regulators on companies with inadequate privacy programs are significant concerns. However, it is essential to consider privacy not just for future legal enforcement but also for present decisions impacting trust and safety. A personal example illustrates the potential consequences of neglecting privacy and safety implications in product development. The story underscores the importance of prioritizing privacy, safety, and user trust, emphasizing the need for proactive measures beyond legal requirements to ensure business efficiency and compliance readiness.

Privacy and regulations

Data functions as both an asset and a liability, affecting not only your reputation but also your financial standing. Understanding the regulatory landscape is crucial, as privacy regulations carry legal weight and non-compliance can result in substantial financial penalties. Access to legal guidance is beneficial for shaping a robust privacy program. Exploring the origins of specific privacy laws, like the Video Privacy Protection Act (VPPA) initiated in 1988, demonstrates the lasting impact and unforeseen consequences of privacy-related decisions. This historical example underscores the potential long-term consequences of privacy laws on contemporary businesses, highlighting the challenges in regulating and implementing policies in today's rapidly evolving technological environment.

Privacy, GDPR, CCPA, and beyond

Industry leaders express significant concerns about privacy regulations, as new laws are continuously emerging. These regulations pose potential threats to their strategic plans and operational capabilities. The EU General Data Protection Regulation (GDPR), effective since May 25, 2018, is a comprehensive data protection law that replaced national laws within EU member states. Key GDPR changes include an expanded definition of personal data, enhanced rights for EU individuals, mandatory breach notifications, and the introduction of data protection impact assessments. The GDPR emphasizes consent, transparency, and security, imposing fines of up to 4% of annual global turnover for non-compliance.

From a California perspective, the California Consumer Privacy Act (CCPA), effective from January 1, 2020, grants consumer privacy rights and imposes business obligations on personal data collection and sale. The California Privacy Rights Act (CPRA), approved on November 3, 2020, further amends and expands the CCPA. The CPRA introduces new rights, including the correction of inaccurate personal information and restrictions on sensitive data use. Businesses are advised to seek legal counsel to navigate the applicability and consequences of these evolving regulations.

Privacy and security

Security and privacy are closely intertwined, and a breach impacting user data is not only a security violation but also a privacy rights infringement for both employees and customers. Examining recent breaches reveals common vulnerabilities that highlight the need for collaboration between privacy and security teams. Two notable breaches, Target in 2013 and Colonial Pipeline in

2021, underscore the risks associated with weak security measures. Target's breach involved hackers infiltrating the retailer's network through stolen HVAC vendor credentials, emphasizing the importance of securing third-party vendors. The Colonial Pipeline breach resulted from a compromised VPN account lacking multifactor authentication, highlighting the critical role of robust security measures in preventing privacy incidents. These cases emphasize the imperative of safeguarding personal data with strong security practices to avert potential privacy breaches.

Privacy and industry pressure

Legal compliance and industry sentiment are crucial influences on privacy practices. While regulations and enforcement play a significant role, industry stakeholders, such as tech platforms, can exert considerable influence over data handling. Recent changes by Apple illustrate this dynamic, where app developers now need approval to collect and use user data. The shift reflects a growing awareness of user autonomy in deciding data-sharing preferences. Companies relying on extensive data collection faced immediate challenges, impacting their ability to connect users and potentially hindering future product development. This highlights the importance of anticipating and adapting to industry-driven changes, emphasizing the need for a flexible and effective privacy program to navigate evolving privacy landscapes.

Privacy and finance

Trust, regulation, and security are significant factors driving privacy acceptance within a company. The shift toward bottom-up agile development decentralizes decision-making, benefiting various stakeholders but introducing associated costs. This decentralized model grants central IT teams less control over data infrastructure, leading to data replication and dissemination across various systems. Engineers often overlook the costs associated with handling big data, assuming it's free. However, this data incurs expenses related to cloud storage, data protection measures like access control and encryption, and the potential trade-off between data quantity and quality. To address these issues, a comprehensive privacy program becomes essential. By forming partnerships with finance and individual teams concerned with budgets, you can advocate for privacy objectives like data deletion and aggregation without explicitly mentioning privacy. This progressive argument reframes privacy as a cost-effective strategy rather than a mere expense, aligning with the company's financial goals.

Privacy and the board of directors

Privacy is not confined to legal concerns or engineering tools; it extends to business health and governance for the board of directors. The board holds key responsibilities in corporate governance, risk management, and compliance. Corporate governance, as defined by the OECD, involves instilling market confidence and business integrity, crucial for accessing capital. A robust privacy record fosters trust and protects reputation, preventing scenarios like Equifax's downgrade due to data protection failure. Risk management, guided by the ERM framework, aligns with a company's mission, ensures efficient resource use, reliable reporting, and compliance with laws. Privacy efforts contribute to risk assessment matrices, evaluating the likelihood and impact of privacy-related issues.

Compliance, another board responsibility, benefits from privacy programs generating artifacts like training, best practices, and customer-centric designs. These not only build trust but also aid in regulatory compliance and certification against standards. Compliance goes beyond regulations, offering access to privacy-sensitive markets and enterprise customers in sectors like healthcare. However, being compliant is a necessary but insufficient condition for privacy, necessitating ongoing improvement based on practical learnings. To work effectively with the board, educate them about and involve them in the privacy program. Regular check-ins, showcasing wins and near misses, and providing insights into the legal landscape will keep the board informed and ready for potential business impacts. Continuous metric updates demonstrate the program's effectiveness. The overarching lesson is that privacy management involves multidimensional considerations, extending beyond risk to encompass various dimensions.

Build vs. buy

To make a meaningful impact with your privacy program, leveraging tools and automation is essential. Decisions on what tools to build, when to build them, and how to measure effectiveness are crucial. A critical decision often delayed is whether to build privacy tools in-house or buy them from a vendor. The ideal approach is not strictly one or the other but a combination, with trade-offs in the Build vs. Buy debate. Challenges in building privacy tools include a lack of dedicated ownership, insufficient expertise, and instability due to information loss when engineers change teams. To mitigate this, set reasonable expectations, buffer teams with contractors, and address potential instability issues. Privacy tools serve diverse stakeholders, requiring a mix of breadth and depth. While third-party vendors may offer platform solutions, consider a combination of point solutions to address specific use cases effectively.

Changes in a company's operating model, long-term goals, and risk appetite impact tooling, making it essential to involve executive and business leaders in decision-making for responsible, strategic choices. Despite the abundance of third-party solutions, the market is flooded with tools of varying quality. Vet third-party solutions with privacy legal teams and engineers to ensure they align with your needs and standards. Avoid deferring privacy tooling with manual processes, as crisis-driven tool purchases may lead to suboptimal decisions. Plan ahead, conduct research, consult industry peers, and perform proof-of-concept testing before committing to a solution. This balanced approach will help you navigate the Build vs. Buy decision effectively for the benefit of your company and customers.

Decentralized vs. centralized

The choice between building privacy tools in-house or buying third-party solutions is a complex debate, much like the critical decision of structuring your privacy program team – centralized or decentralized. In the modern tech landscape, companies often prioritize depth over breadth, leading to decentralized engineering teams with specialized processes, tech stacks, and release pipelines. While this accelerates innovation, it can result in cross-functional disconnects and downstream privacy issues. Additionally, engineers and product managers, focused on individual deliverables and KPIs, may not prioritize privacy projects critical for compliance and trust.

Decentralized time allocation, an idea occasionally floated, aims to distribute the responsibility of privacy automation across teams. While it fosters shared ownership and knowledge, it requires substantial program management and sustained sponsorship. Engineers often prioritize their features unless there is a top-down mandate, which becomes less effective over time.

A centralized approach, strategically paired with decentralization, is considered more scalable, flexible, and sustainable. For operational tooling, a centralized privacy team can own critical and common use cases, collaborate with legal, compliance, and other teams, and adapt to business needs. Rotations and cross-functional expertise enhance team flexibility.

Simultaneously, a horizontal privacy team consisting of senior leaders from various business domains offers strategic privacy ownership. Acclimating leaders to the privacy domain proactively, maintaining continuous alignment with privacy risks, and involving them in scaling the privacy program are advantages of this model. The flexible approach, with centralized technical operations and decentralized strategic ownership, helps address privacy needs proactively and at scale, moving away from perpetual crisis mode.

The Executive Privacy Working Group (EPWG)

To tackle challenges such as privacy, security, safety, and misinformation, an executive privacy working group (EPWG) is essential. Unlike operational teams, this group, comprising leaders from various domains, doesn't engage in hands-on work but plays a crucial role in executive sponsorship, awareness, and escalations. The EPWG involves leaders from engineering, security, data science, UX, business development, and legal, forming an executive team not directly linked to privacy.

The EPWG addresses the tension between product innovation and data protection prevalent in modern engineering teams. It offers several benefits: creating visibility around collective sponsorship for privacy, obtaining buy-in from leaders for privacy projects, providing sustained participation, and incorporating diverse perspectives.

The EPWG has four key responsibilities: establishing first principles for privacy, handling escalations and decisions, managing resources, and ensuring accountability for outcomes. The first principles guide decision-making and serve as a North Star for leaders. Escalations and decisions involve planning meetings effectively to prevent delays in decision-making. Resourcing is vital for implementing privacy principles, with the EPWG aiding in providing resources and prioritization. Finally, the EPWG collectively owns the outcomes, holding accountability if privacy issues arise.

These senior executive leaders in the EPWG are costly to gather, making it crucial to clearly define their roles and long-term expectations. The EPWG acts as a guiding force, providing political cover for the operational privacy team, which requires some level of centralized enforcement. Detailed examination of the roles and expectations ensures effective utilization of the EPWG's expensive gatherings.

Roles and responsibilities in the EPWG

Outline the roles and responsibilities within your EPWG. The Chief Information Security Officer (CISO) is a crucial EPWG component. Their presence facilitates collaboration on risk assessments and addresses conflicts between security and privacy. While security focuses on external threats, privacy can repurpose some tools for internal governance.

Legal holds a vital role in the EPWG due to the regulatory aspects of privacy. Unlike security's binary nature, privacy involves various nuances. Legal leadership in the EPWG is essential for briefing cross-functional leaders on upcoming legal changes, fostering adaptability, and preventing crises.

Product management's role in the EPWG is exemplified by the Strava case. Strava's fitness app inadvertently exposed military locations. EPWG involvement would question the visibility of features like heat maps, encouraging privacy-safe decisions and preventing potential disasters.

Engineering is pivotal in the EPWG, as it executes the product roadmap. Engineers can either hinder or aid privacy goals, making executive leadership representation crucial. Data science contributes critical insights to the EPWG, connecting the company's roadmap and execution, and necessitates leadership representation.

Business development and sales leadership complete the EPWG, ensuring business growth without compromising privacy. For instance, including sales in the EPWG can help address challenges like re-identifying past customers without violating privacy. Integrating sales leadership in the EPWG ensures alignment with business goals while maintaining data privacy.

The key lesson is that the EPWG acts as a deliberative force, questioning decisions and ensuring privacy considerations across various business functions.

Privacy leadership and the chief privacy officer

Explore the role of the privacy program leader within the Executive Privacy Working Group (EPWG). This leader, often the Chief Privacy Officer (CPO), plays a crucial role in aligning strategic privacy goals with operational execution. The

CPO acts as a bridge between the company's privacy strategy and its practical implementation.

The primary responsibilities of the CPO include:

1. Advocacy: Serving as the primary advocate for privacy across the company, convincing executive leadership of the importance of treating customers and their data with trust and transparency.

2. Benchmarking: Staying informed about industry trends and regulatory sentiments to ensure that privacy considerations are integral to product design.

3. Credibility: Establishing credibility by emphasizing that privacy is not only a matter of principle but is also essential for long-term business success.

The role involves several facets:

1. Translator and Bridge Builder: Connecting different parts of the company to create a cohesive and sensible privacy strategy. Resolving stand-offs among EPWG stakeholders and facilitating collaboration.

2. Actionable Guidance: Converting privacy principles into practical guidance by partnering with other teams to develop standards and artifacts. These standards provide a more tangible interpretation of EPWG's first principles.

3. Educator in Chief: Evangelizing and educating the company about privacy, fostering a privacy-aware culture. The CPO must amplify the message to make privacy a top-of-mind consideration for decision-makers.

In summary, the CPO, as the privacy program leader, plays a pivotal role in shaping and implementing the company's privacy strategy, ensuring alignment between strategic vision and day-to-day operations.

The operating privacy team

The second crucial component of your privacy program is the operational privacy team. This team, guided by the EPWG, will execute tasks essential to achieving measurable privacy goals. It will deliver actionable guidance, tools, and processes for safeguarding data privacy across the company. The operational privacy team has three main mandates: demonstrate compliance, build tools and automation, and respond to external requests such as incidents and law enforcement inquiries.

The team will oversee various work streams, including creating data privacy guidelines, serving as the dedicated privacy engineering team, leading cross-functional privacy improvement efforts, supporting audits, evaluating products for privacy risk, responding to incidents, and providing ongoing training. The operational privacy team will be composed of engineers, compliance experts, program and product managers, and incident response specialists.

Determining where this team reports is crucial. While there are pros to having the Chief Privacy Officer (CPO) report to the Chief Information Security Officer (CISO), leveraging existing relationships and best practices, there are cons, such as potential conflicts between security and privacy. Similarly, reporting to the legal team has its advantages, including alignment on the regulatory landscape, but drawbacks include a perceived lack of technical expertise and the absence of direct security involvement.

Considering these factors, the optimal structure might involve the CPO reporting to the CISO with a dotted line to the Office of the General Counsel. Ultimately, the leader should possess the ability to build programs, collaborate across the organization, influence senior engineering leadership, and prioritize privacy. Focus on building privacy governance capabilities and point solutions under the umbrella of privacy automation or privacy tech.

Data classification

Data is a crucial asset that, when misused, can swiftly turn from an invisible asset on your balance sheet to a public liability, raising questions about the difficulty in protecting it from privacy harms. The challenge arises from technologists and innovators understanding data in relation to their goals without fully appreciating the risks associated with unforeseen combinations and uses of that data. Large volumes of data are often protected using one-size-fits-all tools, emphasizing the critical importance of data classification.

Data classification, ranking data based on privacy risk, is essential. The classification process involves asking questions for each unit of data, such as its type, purpose, significance to customers and business, and potential consequences if mishandled. The operations team must ensure that the classification aligns with EPWG principles, involves legal partnerships for compliance with existing and upcoming laws, and considers data usage before classification.

Partnering with security, IT engineering, data science, and legal, the operations team finalizes data protection requirements. This involves setting access controls and retention timelines based on the sensitivity of the data. The EPWG's organizational structure and relationships benefit the operations team during this process.

Sample classification levels, like restricted and confidential, guide this process. Restricted data, which uniquely identifies individuals and can be joined with other data to identify specific individuals, has tight access controls and shorter retention timelines. In contrast, confidential data, often more aggregated, may have looser access requirements and longer retention timelines.

For practical classification skills, a hands-on exercise involves classifying data related to analyzing medicine purchases for pharmacy planning. Personal patient information falls into the restricted category due to its sensitivity, leading to strict access controls and shorter retention. Redacting names while retaining information about medicine purchases could reclassify the data as confidential, allowing longer retention.

Despite being time-consuming, the data classification process should emphasize perpetual progress over perfection, avoiding analysis paralysis. Having grasped data classification, the next step is a detailed exploration of data inventory.

Data inventory

Data governance, encompassing data classification, data inventory, and policy enforcement, is vital for those involved in security, privacy, or compliance. Data classification tailors' protection strategies based on privacy risk, allowing the creation and enforcement of policies using automation. Data inventory involves labeling and tagging data, making discovery and protection more efficient. It connects data to appropriate protection strategies, ensuring alignment with privacy controls.

Clear criteria for structuring tags include compatibility with external privacy requirements, applicability to all data states, canonical definitions, and machine readability. An example of level one data tags provides a starting point for sensitive data categorization. The syntax for tags involves a regular expression format, distinguishing between business and user data and providing a descriptive name.

Timing is crucial, and categorizing data early in the collection stage enhances privacy enforcement scalability. Waiting until the tail end of the data funnel makes automation challenging due to the sheer volume of data. Early categorization allows agile adjustments to privacy policies, facilitating faster privacy enforcement. Data inventory is not just about privacy but also reflects business maturity, revealing trends and prompting thoughtful data collection. Sound data governance leads to more strategic and risk-aware data practices, contributing to organizational maturity and improved efficiency.

Data sharing

Effective data governance, encompassing classification and inventory, is not just a theoretical checkbox—it enhances data use, efficiency, and customer protection. Data sharing is crucial for business growth but poses privacy risks. Balancing operational needs with privacy controls is essential. Risks of data sharing include loss of control, lack of transparency, varied processing abilities, and delayed understanding of implications. De-risking requires understanding the purpose of sharing, data classification, inventory, anonymization, and continuous risk monitoring. Precision in data sharing should inversely correlate with identifiability.

For privacy-conscious data sharing, precision and sharing should have an inverse correlation. Applying techniques is more effective on classified and inventoried data. Suggestions for safe data sharing include documenting retention policies, deleting identifiers, and insisting on anonymization. Techniques involve managing individual-level data, anonymizing data in memory, and removing or replacing identifiers. For identification needs, a linking table strategy with careful access management is recommended. Real-world scenarios require flexibility in applying smart controls for data sharing, fostering business growth while mitigating inherent privacy risks.

Privacy reviews

Privacy reviews are crucial in the development of tech products. In the modern, regulated space, they ensure that privacy concerns are addressed by specialists throughout the innovation process. Two key steps in a comprehensive privacy review process are the Privacy Impact Assessment (PIA) conducted by legal teams and a more technical review by privacy engineers. The PIA focuses on identifying and mitigating privacy risks related to personally identifiable information (PII) collection, purpose, and handling. The technical review, conducted by specialists, occurs early in the product design phase and alongside the PIA process. This shift-left approach involves embedding privacy controls into the design, guiding engineers to implement privacy-safe practices, and collaborating proactively throughout the product development cycle for a more strategic approach to privacy reviews and remediations.

Third-party risk assessment

For effective business growth, companies often need to develop new capabilities, buy existing ones, or employ a combination of both. In the modern corporate landscape, third-party collaborations are common, involving various services like enterprise email, expense management, and travel booking. While convenient, these partnerships come with inherent risks, and companies must treat third-party risks with the same seriousness as internal risks, as regulators and customers may hold them accountable for privacy issues arising from third-party engagements. Companies frequently engage with third parties to fulfill specific needs, yet these external entities may lack the necessary privacy controls, leading to breaches and mistakes that compromise sensitive data.

The growing and porous perimeter of third-party dependencies requires continuous risk management. Key areas to focus on in third-party risk management include developing a defined, documented, and tracked process that covers all business workflows, prioritizing and segmenting privacy fixes for the entire supply chain, serving as an outside auditor for third parties, and facilitating the onboarding and scalable growth of new third parties. A robust privacy program not only mitigates risks but also identifies redundancies and cost-saving opportunities, contributing to business flexibility and forward-thinking growth.

Data deletion

Data, unlike diamonds, should not last forever. Failure to delete data in a timely manner poses risks of external breaches and internal misuse. Keeping unnecessary data incurs storage costs and may hinder the effectiveness of AI models. To address this, deletion involves physically or logically destroying identifiable user data or anonymizing it to prevent re-identification. Best practices for deletion encompass covering various systems and aligning the engineering implementation with publicly disclosed deletion policies. Regulatory requirements, such as GDPR and CCPA, emphasize the need for companies to delete data based on specific circumstances. Collaboration between operational privacy and legal teams is crucial for defining and implementing a deletion policy that is comprehensible across the company and enforceable at scale. Key decisions include choosing a central deletion tool or decentralized deletion by teams, each with its strengths and weaknesses. Challenges arise in preserving data for tax and litigation purposes and dealing with "zombie data" with unknown origins. A cohesive data governance initiative facilitates data categorization, classification, and, consequently, deletion.

Data export

Privacy laws often grant users the right to request their data, necessitating automated data export capabilities. Beyond compliance, trust is a crucial factor, as customers want transparency about their data usage. The risk lies in potential misuse, where dissatisfied customers or activists may exploit export capabilities, overwhelming the company with requests. Automation is essential, but authentication of the requester is equally important to prevent misuse. Data export involves one-way decisions, and without proper authentication and governance, it can be expensive and error-prone. Data governance, including classification and inventory, should precede any export to ensure accuracy. Regulatory requirements include the right to data deletion and the right to access one's data. Consistency in governance tools is vital to avoid privacy failures. Consideration of platforms for data handoff, with cost and security trade-offs, is crucial. Governments may also request customer data export, raising additional considerations around user safety and human rights. While data export is complex, planning and implementation can mitigate challenges.

Consent management

Consent management, like data export, is a vital privacy requirement that balances user trust and regulatory compliance. Automation of consent management is strongly recommended to navigate the complexities effectively. In the era of data-driven development, increased data collection capabilities have led to customer trust issues, privacy mistakes, and the introduction of new privacy laws. Contrary to popular belief, the GDPR does not mandate consent for all business purposes, but obtaining customer permission is a straightforward approach to compliance. Apple's App Store now requires developers to seek user permission before tracking across apps and websites, emphasizing the significance of consent. A Consent Management Platform

(CMP) becomes crucial for compliance, enabling businesses to inform users about data collection and seek specific consents through disclosures.

CMPs have front-end and back-end components, impacting users directly and managing consent tracking complexities, respectively. The back-end of a CMP involves mapping consents to specific disclosures, handling different locations, languages, and versions, and addressing scenarios where users offer and withdraw consent. Data governance and privacy tools are interconnected, emphasizing the need for a well-supported CMP. Backend considerations include managing diverse consent disclosures, mapping to products, updating and storing multiple versions, and handling user consent changes. Despite its complexity, ensuring correct consent handling is critical for user data collection, and building a well-considered CMP is essential for success.

User transparency features

Privacy encompasses more than just legal compliance; it also involves building and maintaining customer trust. Many companies struggle to achieve this trust despite significant privacy investments. The challenge lies in the complexity of privacy policies that are often difficult for non-lawyers, including customers, to comprehend. Additionally, privacy tools running in the background may be invisible to users. To address this, the proposed solution is user transparency, adding a fourth outcome to the typical privacy program structure. This includes principles reflecting company values, compliance-enabling policies, backend tooling for operationalizing privacy compliance, and a user-facing tool for transparency. The user-facing tool serves two purposes: helping users understand what data the company collects and how it's used, and empowering them to control how their data is handled.

This transparency strategy builds trust by providing customers with visibility and authority over their data, reinforcing the message that teams can unite to deliver privacy and efficiency. The approach yields benefits such as direct customer feedback on privacy programs, acknowledgment of backend compliance tools, and the opportunity to view privacy as a customer product rather than a regulatory burden. By incorporating customer feedback, companies can productize privacy, tailor strategies to customer expectations, and demonstrate a return on investment. Transparency features, especially when combined with established data governance, enable companies to gain credit for their privacy investments and foster user trust.

Privacy metrics

Privacy metrics are essential because, despite executive commitment to privacy and security, limited resources can hinder privacy effectiveness. Treating privacy as a product with stakeholders (company, customers, accountability mechanisms) is crucial. Metrics should focus on coverage, data footprint reduction, privacy-sensitive access controls, and user-facing transparency tools. These metrics help assess program effectiveness, secure resources, and demonstrate ROI. Two models guide resource allocation: one emphasizes foundational elements and automation, dedicating 80% of resources, while the second tracks program maturity by monitoring incidents, reviews, and strategic investments. Tactical dashboards, measuring user sentiment through metrics like opt-outs and data requests, enable continuous improvement and proactive program tracking.

Chapter 4 Data Classification and Inventory

Data classification as part of data governance

You might have come across the term "data governance" in discussions on security and privacy. It's essential to truly understand this concept, especially when dealing with customer data and critical assets. Data governance involves collecting, identifying, tracking, and protecting customer and business data. It includes risk analysis, policies, and tools for consistent enforcement at scale. For privacy, effective data governance ensures that privacy and innovation complement each other. Data classification, a continuous and iterative process, identifies privacy risks in individual and combined data, allowing protection with risk-appropriate tools and processes. Collaborative efforts among various stakeholders are crucial for successful data classification. Moreover, data classification serves broader purposes such as security, protecting intellectual property, ensuring data efficiency and quality, and managing storage costs. Recognizing this broader scope positions privacy as a business enabler, fostering growth and trust.

The legal and regulatory landscape

Interested in privacy but finding privacy laws confusing? You're not alone. Disclaimer: I'm not a lawyer, so nothing here is legal advice. Now, a joke: What's the difference between a good lawyer and a great lawyer? A good lawyer knows the law; a great lawyer knows the judge. Privacy laws aren't that amusing, but they are rapidly changing. Key facts: GDPR, enacted in May 2018, set data protection requirements, expanded personal data scope, gave Europeans control over their data, and defined legitimate interests. In the US, states are taking the lead; CCPA, effective January 1, 2020, grants California consumers privacy rights. CPRA (CCPA 2.0) was approved on November 3, 2020, amending and expanding CCPA. Washington Privacy Act (WPA) mirrors GDPR and was introduced in January 2019. Illinois's BIPA deals with biometric data, a concern as more companies collect such information. India, Brazil, and other countries are also considering complex privacy laws. Businesses face two challenges due to these developments.

Privacy regulations and ambiguity

As a consumer, I desire privacy laws safeguarding my data. As a tech executive reliant on customer data for growth, I value robust privacy laws, contrary to misconceptions that companies disregard them. Business success hinges on trust, requiring clear, practical privacy laws. Complex or conflicting laws hinder implementation, impeding innovation without enhancing privacy. In the US and overseas, no universal approach to sensitive data exists, fostering a lose-lose dynamic. Data classification is crucial, yielding defined privacy risks, adaptable definitions for diverse laws, and fostering ongoing collaboration for tailored protections. This approach ensures adaptable privacy governance and empowers engineers and innovators to focus on product development without navigating complex regulations.

Privacy laws and security

Privacy and security, often considered interchangeable, are distinct yet closely linked. Security is essential for privacy, but tools vital for security can complicate privacy protection. Data classification is crucial as it factors in security concerns, aiding in data protection and mitigating internal misuse. For instance, in an app collecting phone numbers and IP addresses, balancing security and product team access, user awareness, avoiding mission creep, and ensuring transparent data collection and access management become critical considerations. The global complexity of the security-privacy relationship underscores the importance of classification in safeguarding customers while fostering business growth. Examples like the impact of GDPR on WHOIS data and potential security issues with data erasure rights highlight the intricate balance needed. We will guide you in addressing these challenges by classifying and inventorying data for privacy preservation with usability intact.

Privacy and the user

Amid discussions on big data and privacy laws, the user stands as the paramount element, driving data, engagement, monetization, and growth. Prioritizing user experience while implementing privacy tools is crucial. Intelligent data classification can strike a balance between user experience and privacy protections. Consider a streaming service facing a privacy law mandating data deletion upon subscription cancellation. While maximizing privacy, it overlooks user behavior complexities, such as returning after a short cancellation period. Customizing data classification to align with business needs and user behaviors is essential. For instance, classifying data based on user tenure enables privacy compliance and business continuity simultaneously, fostering a governance strategy that is both privacy-sensitive and user-friendly.

How classification reduces risk around unstructured data

Data classification and inventory provide crucial advantages for companies, such as insights into the usage patterns of a distributed engineering community, continuous alignment with data protection laws, and the ability to customize data protection tools. Many companies lack processes for managing data collection, posing risks, especially for unstructured data, which comprises a significant and growing portion of stored data. With approximately 80% of collected data being unstructured, effective management becomes vital. Tools powered by artificial intelligence now enable analysis of unstructured data, making it valuable for organizations. Without proper data management, companies risk underutilizing collected unstructured data, falling behind competitors, and incurring unnecessary costs. A robust data governance strategy, encompassing unstructured data, is essential for business competitiveness and addresses privacy, security, and cost concerns. Initiating a data governance program involves three key steps: data classification and governance standards, data inventory, and enforcement of data privacy tools and standards, forming the foundation for "privacy by data."

How can data classification help you?

When initiating early data governance programs, C-level leaders raised two concerns: the belief that existing data was sufficient and no problems had arisen, and the perception of having too much data already. To address these, it's crucial not to succumb to analysis paralysis or wait for a magic solution. Instead, emphasize to the C-suite that data governance is about organizational maturity, transitioning from uncertainty to risk. Data governance helps convert uncertainty into quantifiable risk, enabling identification, quantification, and management of risk through controls. The objective of a privacy program is to facilitate ethical and risk-aware innovation. As a privacy leader, the focus should be on determining necessary actions for the company and executing them with minimal data usage. A continuously refreshed data classification process is essential for developing privacy and risk management tools aligned with the evolving business landscape.

Data classification as part of data governance

Data classification facilitates a deterministic and data-driven access management program, showcasing the importance of sound data governance over shortsighted decisions. Privacy programs can adopt two distinct access management models: a lockdown approach and a three T model (tooling, trust, and training). While the lockdown model involves strict controls, it may impede business efficiency. The three T model combines tools, training, and trust to establish a culture honoring customer data privacy. The optimal approach often integrates elements of both models, locking down extremely sensitive data while applying proportional protections based on risk and use cases for other data. To address the challenge of verifying user identity for sensitive data access, authentication (AuthN) and authorization (AuthZ) tools play a crucial role. Data classification enhances the strategic, thoughtful, and selective deployment of AuthN and AuthZ tools, particularly in the context of the DevOps model. It enables the implementation of role-based access controls, secure management of access keys, generation of audit reports for regulatory compliance, handling SSH keys and secrets, and gaining visibility into cloud systems and access. Applying AuthZ selectively based on data classification ensures a practical and efficient approach to access management.

How to shape the data classification process

To establish an effective end-to-end data classification process, collaboration among various stakeholders, including privacy legal, privacy engineers, security, engineering, product management, and data scientists, is crucial. While privacy is often viewed as a legal domain, relying solely on the legal team for data classification can be a mistake. Instead, a collaborative approach involving legal, engineering, product management, and data science is optimal. The process involves:

1. Working with privacy legal to understand their data classification perspective.

2. Simultaneously collaborating with engineering, product management, and data science to grasp their operational and analysis needs.

3. Creating an initial classification based on legal and operational insights.

4. Opening the draft for company-wide review to address disagreements among key stakeholders.

This collaborative approach ensures that differing opinions on the privacy sensitivity of specific data elements are addressed. For instance, engineering may see certain internal data IDs as non-sensitive, while legal may identify potential privacy concerns. Bridging such gaps involves applying techniques to restrict access based on necessity. Additionally, diverse interpretations of concepts, such as encryption adequacy, can be resolved through collaboration. The key outcome is breaking down silos and fostering partnerships, leading to a more accurate understanding of risk and its comprehensive management for the entire business.

Thought experiment: A sequential data classification

Is it possible to conduct data classification sequentially, with the legal team classifying data first and the technical team handling implementation details afterward? Despite the apparent organization, this approach is not recommended. Collaborative efforts involving all teams are essential for effective data classification. Previous attempts at sequential classification faced inefficiency and prolonged timelines. Privacy culture thrives on shared context among diverse teams, and attempting to separate them hinders collective progress. Disconnecting legal and engineering teams leads to inefficiencies and misinterpretations. Instead, advocate for a continuous, collaborative data classification process. Although it may require more time initially, having all teams involved simultaneously fosters mutual learning and scalability. Moving forward, beyond data classification, protecting data involves applying classification to both future and existing data—a process known as data inventory, the next step in data governance.

What is data inventory?

Data inventory is essentially a comprehensive record of data across all storage systems. Imagine organizing a messy stack of books into a library to make it searchable and usable. To conduct a meaningful data inventory, effective tagging is crucial. The data classification exercise can serve as a starting point for this tagging process, providing information about the data and its associated risks. The classification tags should fulfill multiple purposes, such as aligning with external regulatory requirements (e.g., GDPR, CCPA) and supporting ongoing changes in regulations without constant tag edits. Collaboration with the legal team ensures that tags remain relevant and operational as laws evolve. Additional considerations for tags include applicability to all data states (at rest, in transit, in use), canonical and machine-readable definitions, and versatility for individual or grouped use (e.g., for a column or an entire dataset). Data inventory, when integrated into overall data governance, becomes a crucial aspect of managing data effectively.

Data inventory and data governance

Data privacy and business maturity hinge on effective governance, encompassing risk understanding and mitigation. While data classification reveals risks, it's not enough on its own. This brings us to data inventory, a tool aligning privacy risk with control systems to mitigate that risk. Consider implementing encryption for sensitive data in a retail business, such as email addresses and physical addresses. Balancing privacy and efficiency, you might use a single encryption layer for addresses in large cities, changing keys frequently to deter misuse. For addresses in small towns, multiple encryption layers with less frequent key changes can strike a balance between initial security and legitimate access. Scaling this process for vast amounts of data points, programs, and users necessitates data inventory, facilitating automated governance at scale. This approach avoids trade-offs between data privacy and business efficiency or data protection and innovation. Key building blocks for data inventory, such as creating templates and tags, will be explored to deepen our understanding.

How can you prep for data inventory?

Two key steps for a smooth data inventory setup involve categorizing data by storage systems and data owners. For data categorized by storage systems, use a template that identifies each storage unit (e.g., Hive, Kafka, SQL databases) and attributes like storage size, structured vs. unstructured data percentage, data classification tier, and whether it contains personal data. However, since storage systems are often owned by multiple stakeholders, it's essential to also categorize data by data owner. This template includes attributes such as total size, unit count, structured vs. unstructured, classification tier, and personal data indication. The term "data owner" refers to the person or team accountable for protecting and using the data in line with user expectations. Creating effective tags is crucial, representing the link between data classification, privacy risk, and associated controls. Examples of tag configurations and reduction techniques consist in character choice (underscore, hyphen) for separators. With this foundation, the next step is to establish the necessary infrastructure and architecture for data inventory implementation.

Data inventory using manual resources and automation

Applying tags to reflect privacy risk in the vast and dispersed landscape of data collected by companies poses challenges. A crucial decision in the data inventory process involves resource allocation, specifically determining the balance between manual and automated efforts. Many companies erroneously view this as an either/or choice, often lacking the necessary human labor or automation capabilities for a scalable data inventory. Instead of getting stuck in indecision, adopt an approach that provides flexibility and a starting point. Two options are available: using automation for tagging and manual verification, or initiating manual categorization followed by automation.

A combination of these approaches is advisable, allowing optimization based on available resources. If dedicated privacy experts are present but engineering automation resources are lacking, start with manual categorization, focusing on high-risk and frequently used data sets. Use this baseline to automate the remaining data sets. Conversely, if engineering resources outweigh privacy resources, create basic automation for some data sets, verify categorization with legal input, and iteratively tag the remaining data. The goal is to establish a continuous cycle of tagging, verification, and refinement, aligning with the overall governance strategy. Data inventory and data classification not only contribute to building data governance but also share similar execution cadences. With this approach, you should now have a clear and actionable plan to initiate your data inventory process.

The technical implementation of data inventory

To implement data inventory, you need a backend infrastructure that performs key functions: crawling various known data stores, discovering additional data stores, especially around unstructured data, making data sets and metadata available for tagging, supporting the addition of new metadata, and facilitating the categorization of personal data for privacy-specific purposes. Breaking down the architecture, the initial steps involve crawling known data stores, discovering data sets, and making them available for tagging. Given the prevalence of unstructured data, tools like crawlers are essential to explore various data stores and apply tags at the right granularity. The need for tools arises because engineers and data scientists might not always be aware of the data they collect, especially in cases like JSON blobs.

Moving forward, the infrastructure should provide extensibility for engineers to add new metadata in a self-service manner. While engineers may not perform end-to-end data inventory, providing them the option to input relevant information through an API or UI is beneficial. The process of entering data information can be facilitated by engineers, contributing to the overall success of the inventory program.

Next, the infrastructure must support the categorization of personal data. After discovering data, applying tags becomes crucial, requiring a combination of infrastructure, automation, human judgment, and potentially artificial intelligence. The entire data inventory process can be costly, but steps one through four are necessary for data science teams to enhance data quality and discovery, making the investment worthwhile.

Data inventory architecture

Create the backend system architecture for data inventory. Configuration is essential to adapt this system to your company's needs. The data inventory service (DIS) in box number one is where data inventory occurs, adding tags to data based on its classification. Going forward, we'll refer to this service as DIS. Incoming data, represented by box number two, is made available for the inventory service through crawlers, event listeners, and other tools in box number three. The data classification process, box number four, involves cross-functional teams classifying data based on regulations, usage, and risk. Machine-readable tags are created in box number five, as we saw in earlier examples.

The data inventory process is analogous to a grand buffet, comprising data to be inventoried, classification based on risk, machine-readable tags for implementation, and business logic for affixing tags. The DIS service inventories data. Completing the data inventory process before operational or analytical usage is crucial.

In the technical walkthrough, step one involves consolidating data and metadata using crawlers and listeners. Step two, manual and automated data categorization, focuses on manual categorization for training ML models and ML-driven classification to reduce reliance on manual processes. Step three, deciding on data classification, finalizes tagging after manual and ML-driven efforts.

The DIS service functions as both a service and a database. As a service, it feeds data to manual and ML-based classifiers. Simultaneously, DIS, as a database, provides information to classifiers for automatic inference, enabling both manual and automated classification. DIS stores the tagged data in a separate temporary database, facilitating judgment checks before applying policies for protection. This marks the end-to-end process of data classification, data inventory, and applying protection techniques tailored to data risk, extending privacy by design into what I term "privacy by data."

Creating the Backend System Architecture for Data Inventory

1. Data Inventory Service (DIS):

   - The DIS service is the core of the data inventory architecture, responsible for tagging data based on its classification.

   - This service is integral to the entire process and will be referred to as DIS going forward.

2. Incoming Data:

   - Data from various sources is made available for the inventory service through crawlers, event listeners, and other tools.

3. Data Collection Tools:

   - Crawlers, event listeners, and other tools collect and consolidate data, along with its metadata, for the inventory process.

4. Data Classification Process:

   - Cross-functional teams collaborate in the classification process, considering regulations, usage, and risk.

5. Machine-Readable Tags:

   - Automated creation of machine-readable tags based on the classification process.

6. Data Inventory Process:

   - Analogous to a grand buffet, this process involves:

     - Data collection for inventory.

     - Classification based on risk.

     - Implementation of machine-readable tags.

     - Application of business logic for affixing tags.

7. Technical Walkthrough:

   - Step 1: Consolidate data and metadata using crawlers and listeners.

   - Step 2: Manual and automated data categorization:

     - Manual categorization for training ML models.

     - ML-driven classification to reduce reliance on manual processes.

   - Step 3: Decide on data classification, finalizing tagging after manual and ML-driven efforts.

8. DIS Service Functions:

   - As a Service: Feeds data to manual and ML-based classifiers.

   - As a Database: Provides information to classifiers for automatic inference.

   - Stores tagged data in a separate temporary database for judgment checks before applying protection policies.

9. End-to-End Process:

- Completion of the data classification process, data inventory, and application of protection techniques tailored to data risk.

- Extends the concept of "privacy by design" into "privacy by data."

Data inventory metadata

Successful data inventory infrastructure requires two critical attributes. First, it needs a comprehensive way to capture metadata for accurate data classification. Second, it requires consistent metadata definitions across all data sources. To implement such infrastructure, DIS should encompass not only datasets but all data entities, covering online, offline, and real-time datasets, as well as other data artifacts like ML features, business metrics, and dashboards. Additionally, it should gather information from services, including data lineage and other infrastructure components. This investment emphasizes the need for companies to allocate infrastructure resources to manage data based on its nature and associated privacy and security risks.

To handle metadata and ensure accurate classification, a recommended approach is to use a taxonomy-like structure with entity and value types in the backend. This allows standardization of metadata from online schemas to offline Hive database schemas, services, and storage-level components.

In the metadata collection process, a model involving both pull and push models is suggested. Crawlers, acting as pull models, can periodically collect information from metadata sources, while event-based listeners offer near real-time collection for time-sensitive information. On the push model side, making APIs available to pipelines and services, as well as using crowdsourcing for human-generated information, contributes to a comprehensive metadata collection strategy. This approach is crucial given the vast volume and diversity of data handled by most companies.

Data inventory and use cases

There's no one-size-fits-all approach to how deeply you should conduct data inventory in your stack. While it's a complex task that shouldn't be redone frequently, it's crucial not to rush through it. Different companies use various storage models for their data. The following models can be customized based on your needs, risk tolerance, and budget.

1. Level One Inventory:

- Operates at the database or application instance level.

- Provides total data store size and tags data.

- Key Performance Indicators (KPIs) measure outcomes as a percentage of total volume.

- Goals: Understand data source composition, identify data sources, and apply controls.

2. Level Two Inventory:

  - Builds on Level One but goes a bit deeper.

  - Operates at the column level for databases and data centers.

  - Tags data at the data object level for cloud data.

  - Increased complexity and cost compared to Level One.

  - Goals: Deeper understanding of data sources, enhanced education and data minimization, and improved data protection.

3. Level Three Inventory:

  - Transforms the entire data store into an indexed database.

  - Provides control over customer data for download and deletion.

  - Addresses requirements of GDPR, CCPA, and CPRA.

  - Enables targeted processing of data components.

  - Necessary for compliance with privacy laws and avoiding massive hardware investments.

Each level offers increasing clarity about your data, allowing for better protection at scale. Level Three Inventory, in particular, is crucial for complying with modern privacy laws, enabling individual targeting for deletion, encryption, and portability without massive hardware investments in distributed systems.

Evaluating data inventory outcomes

Data inventory encompasses architecture, business logic, services, and tools. Machine learning (ML) plays a key role in the tagging process based on predefined rules. Unlike data classification, which involves rule creation without real data application, data inventory involves real-time tagging of large data volumes, considering data understanding, source, and downstream use. Using ML for tagging entails trade-offs, considering variables like data volume, available training data, and critical metrics such as performance and accuracy. Tagging should be storage-agnostic and consistent at the column/field level. An example table demonstrates trade-offs in accuracy, performance, and coverage among different ML models. It's crucial to address false positives and balance accuracy and performance, emphasizing the need for early and strategic investment in inventory to avoid rushed, error-prone processes after privacy issues arise. Strategic planning and a cross-functional approach are essential, emphasizing the importance of avoiding shortcuts and panic-inducing situations.

Centralized vs. decentralized

As your data inventory efforts expand, a crucial strategic question arises: whether to build a central architecture or provide automation and logic to decentralized teams for customization. Both options have drawbacks, so careful consideration is necessary. The centralized model initially reduces the burden on decentralized teams and facilitates continuous improvement based on collective feedback. However, it risks imposing a one-size-fits-all categorization process that may not align with specific business needs, leading to a lack of ownership by decentralized teams during issues. On the other hand, delegating categorization to decentralized teams allows each to optimize for velocity and accuracy independently. However, this approach may create silos, hindering a comprehensive business-wide understanding of data and risk. Balancing these trade-offs requires ongoing adaptation and improvisation in your strategy.

Data inventory successes

Given the significant workload and investment involved in data governance, measuring its effectiveness may take time before noticeable data-driven improvements in business practices emerge. To assess the strategy's success, consider the following anecdotal and cultural indicators based on years of experience in the domain:

1. Data Protection Cost: Evaluate when the cost of protecting data becomes excessively high due to an overwhelming volume. Effective data governance should lead to more selective and thoughtful data collection, reducing the need for excessive security and storage expenses.

2. Data Deletion Capability vs. Collection Capability: Assess the balance between your ability to delete data at scale and your ability to collect data at scale. Sound governance should result in timely data deletion and anonymization, minimizing the risk associated with data accumulation.

3. Discovery of Hidden Data: Identify the inflection point when you stop discovering data hidden by engineers or scientists. A reduction in such discoveries suggests improved data handling practices and cultural changes within the company.

4. Impact on Data Quality: Examine the role of privacy in enhancing data quality and assess collaboration opportunities with teams like data science and platform teams. Improved data handling practices and a mature privacy culture may lead to fewer surprises and collaborative efforts to reduce data size.

Monitoring these factors will provide insights into the effectiveness of your data governance strategy, indicating positive changes in data practices and cultural awareness within the organization.

Data inventory challenges

Understanding the difficulty of data inventory goes beyond technical aspects. In various settings, including seminars and conferences, the challenge is often questioned. Here are the key reasons:

1. Delayed Emphasis on Privacy: Privacy efforts typically lag behind company growth, with privacy specialists brought in after incidents or fines. Growth fuels privacy initiatives, and specialists need to collaborate with, not oppose, the business.

2. Decentralized Growth: Companies, in their early stages, prioritize decentralized growth, resulting in independent teams with their own tech stacks and data practices. This approach, termed "democratized and decentralized development," leads to inconsistent data handling across teams, hindering a comprehensive understanding of customers and legal requirements.

3. Privacy Requires Consistency: Privacy demands a consistent approach, irrespective of user location or team-specific challenges. A sophisticated privacy program is necessary, requiring a different mindset than the growth-focused one.

4. Procrastination: Many companies delay implementing privacy programs until a major incident or legal action occurs. Waiting amplifies data and risk, necessitating urgent fixes. Some engineers may resist change, sticking to familiar practices, leading the company to resemble a data addict reluctant to confront the consequences of past actions.

Recognizing these challenges is crucial for effective data governance, emphasizing the need for a proactive and consistent approach to privacy.

Getting executive buy-in for data inventory

In facing potential resistance from executives regarding data inventory, employing a balanced approach is essential. The stick in this case involves using resources like www.enforcementtracker.com, showcasing fines imposed globally for insufficient data governance. Visual aids, such as illustrating the persistence of data breaches over time, emphasize the limitations of relying solely on security tools.

Highlighting that privacy challenges extend beyond big tech companies, especially for startups pre-IPO, addresses a systemic disconnect. Privacy laws, tailored for individualized user rights, clash with the design of modern decentralized systems built for mass data handling. The beauty of unstructured data, while beneficial for rapid growth, introduces challenges in ensuring privacy compliance.

Presenting data inventory to executives involves strategic planning. Utilizing a template, data volume, and the percentage posing risks for each source can be communicated effectively. Key considerations include aligning data growth with customer base and revenue, identifying teams responsible for data growth, and balancing cost reduction with risk management. The goal is to centralize business insights and prevent data and risk from outpacing management capabilities, emphasizing the crucial role of data governance in protecting the business and respecting user data.

Chapter 5 Data Sharing

Data classification as part of data governance

Like data classification, ensuring the privacy of our data sharing is a crucial aspect of data governance. Strategic and thoughtful planning is essential due to the critical role data sharing plays in the modern economy. When viewed through a data sharing lens, data governance involves identifying, tracking, and protecting customer and business data. It encompasses risk analysis, the establishment of policies to manage those risks, and the implementation of tools to consistently enforce those policies at scale. Data classification serves as the foundational starting point for governance. Without proper data classification, there's a risk of inadequate or excessive processes and tools, which is even more pronounced in the context of data sharing. Given the substantial volumes of data, the contextual nature of privacy, and the irreversible nature of data sharing, integrating data governance into your data sharing strategy is crucial.

When dealing with data sharing, considerations must be made for risks such as sharing data without consent, high-volume data sharing without tracking, and insufficient monitoring of data protection after it leaves the security perimeter. Sound data governance allows for legitimate data sharing without compromising privacy. Building on the foundation laid by data classification and data inventory, data sharing involves mapping privacy risk to protection methodologies like access management and encryption. Classification aids in implementing techniques such as anonymization, obfuscation, coarsening, differential privacy, etc., enabling control over privacy risks by modifying or protecting data before and during sharing. The choice of techniques may depend on various factors, including the nature of the data, the tools used for sharing, the recipients, their maturity, credibility, and other relevant considerations. In this sense, data sharing benefits from data governance, just as data classification contributes to creating effective data governance.

How data sharing works: The ads use case

Examine the mechanics of data sharing through the concrete example of online advertising. Although opinions on online advertising may vary, understanding its complexities can shed light on data sharing and its privacy implications. The Electronic Frontier Foundation conducted research illustrating the fundamental process of how internet ads are served. A publisher is a website that displays ads, such as the New York Times website or app. A supply-side platform (SSP) is an ad network helping decide which advertiser can display ads on a website. Conversely, a demand-side platform (DSP) collaborates with SSPs to present ads to users when they visit webpages or apps.

The data flow starts with your browser sending information to SSPs, usually in the form of a cookie. The SSP creates a bid request based on your past behavior, forwarding it to advertisers (DSPs) interested in displaying ads. The bid request contains sensitive information like location, interests, and device ID. Despite being crucial for deciding whether to show an ad, it's essential to remember that behind this data is a real person who deserves trust, privacy, and transparency. Advertisers may bid based on the request, and the SSP selects a winner, displaying the ad on the website.

It's crucial to note that this process occurs without many users comprehending the backend workings, and data is shared before bids or winners are determined. There's no guarantee that a bidding company intends to display an ad; they might seek data for other purposes. Given the powerful nature of data sharing, consumers require tools to protect their privacy, highlighting the need for privacy-preserving techniques in any data sharing.

Data sharing risks: A case study

Explore a case study to grasp the tangible privacy risks associated with data sharing. Data sharing extends beyond company-to-company exchanges; any instance of data leaving your company involves sharing information with external entities. Identifying individuals has become increasingly effortless due to publicly available data, dark web information, and machine learning tools. To illustrate, the New York Times Privacy Project revealed that real-time location data from mobile apps can potentially track anyone, including public figures like the President. In a specific example, the Times de-anonymized location data of President Trump, showcasing how location sharing can be exploited. This case emphasizes that data sharing, when combined with other available data, can be both effective and problematic. Subsequent examples, such as the Cambridge Analytica scandal and ransomware attacks, underscore the importance of understanding the implications of data sharing. Once data leaves your company, control diminishes, and shared data can be mishandled by entities with more sophisticated capabilities.

When data sharing should raise red flags

Privacy risks related to data sharing are dynamic and subject to change due to various factors. The data itself, third-party data, contextual elements, and the ability to identify users through automation can all undergo modifications before, during, and after the sharing process. Privacy risks fluctuate due to unpredictable and challenging-to-manage factors. To address these concerns, app designers focusing on data sharing need to be vigilant for specific red flags. These include:

1. Uniquely identifying individuals without adequate anonymization of the data.

2. Tracking individuals' specific locations at particular times.

3. Lack of consent and transparency regarding how data is shared and with whom.

4. The potential to identify individuals connected to the user who may not have consented to data sharing.

For instance, in the context of a mobility app, real-time tracking of a trip with precise start and stop coordinates could raise privacy concerns. Privacy guidelines from the data recipient are also crucial. Emphasizing the importance of data sharing, it's emphasized that once data is shared, there's no way to retract it. This not only pertains to privacy but also to users' safety. The New York Times research highlights that several companies collect and share location data, emphasizing the need for app developers to incorporate privacy techniques to anonymize data effectively.

Valid reasons for data sharing

While data sharing presents challenges, there are legitimate reasons for apps to share data with external entities. These reasons extend beyond business growth or financial gains. For instance, when using a taxi or ride-sharing app to hail a car, it's probable that the app shares some data with government authorities and transportation providers, such as cab companies. This sharing serves important purposes:

1. Informing Policy Decisions: City planners and regulators may require data from transport providers to make informed decisions and enforce policies related to traffic, parking, emissions, and labor practices.

2. Fee Collection and Safety Enforcement: Municipalities and law enforcement may need data to collect per-vehicle fees, enforce parking regulations for shared bikes and scooters, and address safety or service issues.

Other valid use cases for data sharing include sharing drop-off locations to analyze their impact on parking and traffic flow, sharing trip telemetry data to identify vehicles entering prohibited zones for enforcement citations, and sharing vehicle or driver's license numbers to ensure compliance with city permits.

Techniques to minimize privacy risk

Data sharing poses privacy risks, but adopting best practices can mitigate them. A key principle is that the more precisely identifiable the data, the shorter its retention period should be. This principle aligns with the inverse correlation between precision and retention. As an app designer, request vendors and partners to document retention and deletion policies for each data type. Obfuscate data before sharing, emphasizing that highly identifiable data should have shorter retention. Encourage partners to anonymize data in memory, especially for granular data, making precise data short-lived. Best practices include removing or replacing identifiers before sharing and creating tables to link external identifiers for specific use cases. Custom IDs for vendors are debated, with choices involving hashing or creating internal IDs per vendor. Techniques for sharing location and time data involve adjustments to enhance privacy without compromising aggregate analysis. Monitor partner access to data, limit API availability, and routinely check if granted access is genuinely necessary. Following the principle of "Trust but verify" and embracing a mindset of caution, as stated by Intel Founder Andy Grove, is essential in the world of data sharing for privacy protection.

Anonymization concepts

Anonymization is the process of altering data to reduce the risk of identifying users, locations, or other sensitive information. Personal data includes direct identifiers (e.g., names) and indirect identifiers (e.g., zip codes). Anonymization methods include pseudonymization, which replaces direct identifiers with artificial ones; partial anonymization, involving removal and transformation of identifiers; and full anonymization, ensuring data cannot be linked externally. These techniques help balance privacy risks, compliance obligations, effort, and cost. The chart illustrates that as you move right, privacy risks decrease, but effort and cost increase, presenting trade-offs in data anonymization strategies.

Anonymization techniques

Various anonymization techniques exist, each with trade-offs. Suppression involves removing or withholding data, but it may not lead to full anonymization due to remaining indirect identifiers. Substitution replaces identifiable data with random values, but it may not always achieve full anonymization and can be challenging at scale. Noise addition involves adding random elements to data to disguise individual records, but it has limitations, and semantic viability is crucial. Permutation shuffles attribute values to break correlations, but it must be combined with other techniques and may not provide strong guarantees. Aggregation generalizes data where granularity is unnecessary, but it alone does not ensure full anonymization, requiring additional techniques like k-anonymity.

Encryption

Security and privacy are closely linked, with security tools guarding against external attacks and internal misuse. Encryption serves as a foundational privacy tool with key benefits: it limits data access to authorized individuals, preserves data integrity, authenticates data, and ensures non-repudiation. Robust encryption practices include using secure algorithms, safeguarding secret keys, and distributing public keys through certificates. Cryptography aids in privacy by establishing trust through authentication, identifying data creators, and preventing forgery. When using encryption for data sharing, caution is advised to avoid assumptions, interception proxies, and sharing unnecessary information. A comprehensive data protection strategy, beyond encryption alone, is crucial to thwart specific goals of inappropriate data use. Examining breaches at the Office of Personnel Management (OPM) and Equifax highlights the potential national security risks when combining breached data sets. While encryption is a key tool, it should be applied thoughtfully, considering potential challenges and complemented by a comprehensive data protection strategy.

What is k-anonymity?

Explore k-Anonymity, a concept extensively explored by Professor Latanya Sweeney. In simple terms, k-Anonymity involves suppressing attributes until each row is indistinguishable from at least k-1 other rows, making the database k-anonymous. This approach prevents definitive linkages, ensuring that, at worst, an individual's entry is narrowed down to a group of k individuals. Google utilizes k-Anonymity in their Ad API, offering a guarantee that an individual is part of a minimum cohort rather than uniquely identifiable. By applying k-Anonymity to a raw table, we alter fields to reduce individual uniqueness, exemplifying a k-Anonymity value of 2, indicating increased privacy before data sharing. This technique serves as a powerful tool for assessing privacy impact before sharing data.

How l-diversity helps privacy

To understand the limitations of k-Anonymity, consider a scenario where you achieve a k-Anonymity value of 5. However, if there's a pickup point in your dataset where every trip goes to the same destination, external data could reveal the likely destination for any passenger from that starting point. To address this privacy concern, l-Diversity comes into play. L-Diversity ensures a diversity of potential pickups and drop-offs, requiring that, for each reported trip in a specific time window, a pickup has at least l different potential drop-offs, and every drop-off has at least l potential pickups.

k-Anonymity vs. l-diversity

The tension between security and privacy, as well as between privacy and data quality, is evident. For instance, K-Anonymity may excessively filter out data, but L-Diversity offers a more effective solution. In the diagram, applying a K-Anonymity value of two would filter out every ride due to unique pickups and drop-offs. However, applying an L-Diversity value of two, while separating pickups and drop-offs, preserves the entire dataset and ensures privacy. In scenarios like studying pickup density for improved service, disconnecting pickups and drop-offs enhances data quality, reduces storage costs, and improves privacy. L-Diversity proves beneficial for both internal data storage and external data sharing, showcasing its effectiveness in balancing privacy, data quality, and security in a nuanced manner.

Your physical fingerprint

In various regions globally, the human fingerprint serves as a primary identifier for essential aspects such as accessing government benefits and verifying voting eligibility. In the U.S., providing fingerprints was part of my naturalization process. A paper titled "Unique In the Crowd: The Privacy Bounds of Human Mobility" explores the identifiability of individuals through their human fingerprint, emphasizing the need for 12 points to achieve unique identification. The paper delves into how your digital fingerprint, encompassing location and time data, can be particularly revealing, especially when combined with other available data about your movements.

Your digital fingerprint

In their study analyzing 15 months of human mobility data for 1.5 million individuals, researchers made a significant discovery: human mobility traces are remarkably unique. Spatial-temporal data, indicating your location and time, is highly identifying. For instance, in a dataset detailing individual locations hourly with carrier antenna-level spatial resolution, only four spatial-temporal points were sufficient to uniquely identify around 95% of individuals. Your digital fingerprint, represented by spatial-temporal data, is approximately three times more identifiable than your human fingerprint.

The power of joining outside data

Repeatedly emphasized is the caution that even with attempts to anonymize user data, the potential for identification using external data remains. Skepticism often arises when discussing this at industry events or with engineers. Two examples highlight the potency of outside data against privacy and security controls. In one case, unique pattern in an ostensibly anonymized dataset allowed the linking of information back to an individual, as seen in the Strava example. Another example involves a journalist successfully identifying Senator Mitt Romney's secret Twitter account by cleverly piecing together information about his family and interests. These instances illustrate the efficacy of external data in surpassing traditional privacy measures.

Next steps

Rebuilding public trust for tech companies involves treating data with respect and ensuring responsible data sharing. The techniques discussed in this book aim to safeguard users and their data from misuse by any data-sharing partners. It is recommended to study, test, and implement these techniques, fostering safer data sharing and reducing privacy incidents. As data becomes more anonymized, trust between the tech industry and users can be genuinely restored.